Conversations After a Burial

Yasmina Reza's first play, *Conversations après un
Enterrement*, won her the Best Author Molière Award
and the New Writer Award from the SACD in 1987.
Her work for theatre and cinema includes *La Traversée
de L'Hiver*, *'Art'*, which received the Molière Award
for best play, best production and best author and the
Evening Standard Award and the Olivier Award for
Best Comedy of the Year, a prize-winning adaptation
of Steven Berkoff's version of Kafka's *Metamorphosis*,
and the screenplays *Jascha, Jim Mode Ne Pour Aider*
and *À Demain*.

Christopher Hampton was born in the Azores in 1946.
He wrote his first play, *When Did You Last See My
Mother?*, at the age of eighteen. His work for the theatre,
television and cinema includes *The Philanthropist*,
adaptations from Ibsen and Molière and the screenplays
Dangerous Liaisons, *Carrington* and *The Secret Agent*,
the last two of which he also directed.

by the same author

'ART'

THE UNEXPECTED MAN

HAMMERKLAVIER

YASMINA REZA

Conversations After a Burial

translated by
Christopher Hampton

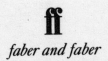

faber and faber

First published in 2000
by Faber and Faber Limited
3 Queen Square London WC1N 3AU

Typeset by Country Setting, Kingsdown, Kent CT14 8ES
Printed in England by Mackays of Chatham plc, Chatham, Kent

A CIP record for this book
is available from the British Library

ISBN 0-571-20441-4

2 4 6 8 10 9 7 5 3 1

Conversations After a Burial was first performed at the Almeida Theatre, London, on 7 September 2000. The cast was as follows:

Nathan Matthew Marsh
Édith Amanda Root
Alex Paul Higgins
Pierre David Calder
Julienne Claire Bloom
Élisa Clare Holman

Director Howard Davies
Designer Rob Howell
Lighting Mark Henderson
Music Dominic Muldowney
Sound John A. Leonard and Fergus O'Hare

Characters

Nathan, 48

Édith, 45

Alex, 43, Nathan and Édith's brother

Pierre, 65, their uncle, their mother's brother

Julienne, 64, his wife

Élisa, 35, Alex's ex-mistress

Setting

The family property in the Loiret.
Nothing realistic.
A single open space.
The woods, the clearing and the house
are simply suggested, with different elements,
so that blackouts, whether during or between
scenes, can be as brief as possible.

Noon.

In the silence of the undergrowth, a man is covering his father's coffin with earth. Then he moves away.

Nathan, Édith and Alex stand, motionless. Pierre and Julienne are further off. Somewhat in the background is Élisa. Nathan takes a piece of paper out of his pocket and reads aloud.

Nathan 'When my mother died, I was six. She was walking upstairs with her suitcase and I can remember the suitcase skidding across the flagstones. When my father passed away, I was eleven and it was war time . . . I found myself alone in the world, so alone and so instantly awake that I was visited by the Devil . . . I welcomed him as a strategic reinforcement, a rampart on my fortress where I could slip away, sheltered from the loopholes. From that day and ever afterwards, I confronted life, bristling with spines from head to toe, stainless and icy. I gave my imaginary son the name of Nathan. For your sake, Nathan, my dazzling spark, may Heaven grant I do not die too soon. Simon Weinberg, 1928.' Dad was twenty.

Blackout.

A terrace. On a level with the house. A table. Some garden chairs. Alex and Nathan, standing.

Nathan Where have you been?

Alex My room.

Nathan I called you, you didn't answer.

Alex Has she gone?

Nathan I don't know.

Alex Who told her?

Nathan I don't know . . .

Alex You did.

Nathan No.

Édith appears.

Édith It was me . . . I told her.

Alex You told her to come?

Édith No. (*Pause.*) What's it matter?

Alex Has she gone?

Édith No.

Alex Tell her to bugger off.

Édith Stop it . . .

Alex Tell her to bugger off. Please.

Silence.

Édith Would you like me to make some coffee?

Alex There's something obscene about it!

Édith Listen, Alex, this isn't quite the moment, don't you think . . .

Nathan Leave him alone.

Édith They saw each other, you know, she even came here without telling you.

Alex So?

Édith I mean, there's nothing abnormal about her being here . . .

Alex I suppose if you go and visit someone, you feel you have to go to their funeral! You poor thing, you must spend your life at funerals!

Nathan Will you make some coffee, Édith?

Édith Yes . . .

Alex Leave it. I'll do it. (*as he goes*) No doubt I'm the one who's abnormal.

Nathan It's your behaviour that's abnormal.

Alex looks at Nathan, then leaves. Édith sits down. Silence.
Élisa appears.

Édith Sit down . . . Come and sit down . . .

Élisa No, I won't stay, thank you . . . I just came to say goodbye . . . Goodbye, Édith . . .

They embrace.

. . . Goodbye, Nathan . . . (*She moves towards him and hesitates, then holds out her hand. She half turns.*)

Nathan Élisa . . .

3

Élisa Yes?

Nathan Stay a while . . .

Édith Alex has gone to make some coffee, stay a little while . . .

Élisa He'll be back . . .

Pause.

Nathan Where's my uncle?

Élisa He's gone down the road for a walk, with his wife.

Nathan Do you know her?

Élisa No.

Nathan Sit down.

Élisa No . . .

Nathan If I sit down, will you sit down?

Élisa No . . .

Alex (*voice-over*) Édith, where are the filter-papers?

Édith Above the sink . . . (*She gets up and leaves.*)

Silence.

Nathan You've cut your hair.

Élisa Yes . . . quite a long time ago.

Nathan It's nice . . .

Élisa You think so?

Nathan Yes.

Élisa I have to go . . .

Silence.

Nathan Goodbye.

Élisa Goodbye. (*She half turns, then moves back towards him. Very quickly*) Nathan, I don't suppose we'll ever see each other again, there's something I have to say to you . . . For years now, I've only had one thing in my mind, to see you again, I've only had one obsession, to see you again, to see you, to hear your voice . . . My life's been haunted by you, I'm incapable of loving anybody else . . .

She turns away and leaves very quickly. Nathan remains, on his own.
Darkness.

Same scene, same lighting. Nathan is alone. Édith appears, carrying coffee cups.

Édith Has she gone?

Nathan Yes.

Edith puts the cups on the table.

Édith Jean just phoned. I almost invited him to lunch tomorrow and then I thought . . . Actually I don't much want to see him, well, not him exactly, but . . . He's been posted to London.

Nathan Is he pleased?

Édith I imagine so. (*She smiles.*) Although he announced it to me in his sinister voice . . .

Nathan smiles.

Aren't you hot? I don't know why I'm so hot . . . (*She takes off her cardigan.*) You'd think it was September . . . She was right to leave.

Alex appears with the coffee-pot.

Alex It'll be weak, I had to scrape the bottom of the packet.

5

Nathan In the cupboard in the pantry?

Alex Didn't look in there.

Édith It's the first time I've seen you make coffee.

Alex How do you imagine I survive?

Édith I didn't say you didn't know how to. You take everything the wrong way.

Alex I don't take everything the wrong way, now what have I said? It's just you seem to think it's some revelation that I know how to make coffee, any idiot knows how to make coffee, it's hardly a bravura feat . . . You already asked me, in the kitchen, if I knew how to do it.

Édith (*upset*) I didn't ask you if you knew how to do it, I asked you if you'd like some help.

Alex Same thing.

Nathan (*while Alex is finishing pouring out the coffee*) Your coffee's piss.

Alex tastes it and puts his cup down with a disgusted expression.

Alex What are the others doing?

Nathan Pierre and his wife have gone for a walk. Élisa's left.

Alex Did you see her?

Nathan She came to say goodbye to us.

Alex Did you ask her to leave?

Nathan No.

Silence. Alex paces.

Alex The vegetable garden needs clearing, it's choked with nettles. (*to Édith*) Are there any secateurs?

Édith You want to clear the vegetable garden with secateurs?!

Alex I can't look at those woods without thinking of Dad suffocating underneath them . . . It's insane to have buried him here . . . Can't you both feel how oppressive it is? I can see his head, his nostrils full of earth, muffled birdsong . . .

Édith Stop it . . .

Nathan The secateurs are in the shed, on the table.

Alex (*turning back towards Édith*) I feel like picking some thistles, you see. Hence the secateurs. (*He leaves.*)

    Pause.

Édith You remember those bouquets of thistles?

Nathan He remembers them.

Édith It's the wrong time of year . . . What shall I make for dinner? There's nothing. A tin of tuna, some rice . . .

Nathan Great.

Édith You think they'll stay this evening?

Nathan No idea.

Édith She's so exhausting . . .

Nathan She's amusing, she's lively . . .

Édith You think so?

Nathan Yes . . . I really like her.

    Pause.

Édith Help me, Nathan.

    Blackout.

A country road. Pierre and Julienne are walking. She's taken off her coat, which she's carrying over her arm.

Julienne If I'd known it was going to be this warm, I'd have worn my gaberdine . . . You must admit, when all's said and done, you couldn't predict this in November! In any event, I can't think why I wore black, ridiculous. I was the only one in black. What are we doing this evening? You think we'll be staying for dinner?

Pierre Might be a bit insensitive to impose on them.

Julienne You see yourself driving back this evening? Couldn't we at least spend the night?

Pierre We'll see.

Julienne The countryside's so boring round here. Not a bit like Normandy. She's pretty, that Élisa. Don't you think?

Pierre Bit flat-chested.

Julienne A bit flat-chested, yes. It's the fashion. Stop. See, it's terrible, I've only got to go fifty yards and I'm gasping.

Pierre You never do any exercise; what do you expect?

Julienne No, no, it's worse than that, there's something the matter with my heart, I'm sure of it. Look, feel . . . Not like that! . . . (*She giggles.*) Really, Pierre, not in the road!

Pierre (*moving his hand around underneath her blouse*) However many layers do you have on?!

Julienne Three, not counting my coat. I put on a thermal vest just before we came out.

Pierre You must be suffocating under all that!

Julienne I am suffocating. It's the thermal vest that's really getting me down.

Pierre Take it off.

Julienne Where? Here?!

Pierre We could find a tree . . .

Julienne You see a tree anywhere?

Pierre If you had any guts, you'd take it off in the cornfield, while I keep watch in the road.

Julienne Suppose the farmer sees me?

Pierre There's no one around.

Julienne You don't know these farmers, one day Nicolas was walking across some field somewhere, and the fellow chased him in his tractor! I'll be all right, I'll be all right, stop fussing.

Pierre We'll go back if you like, you can take it off back there. At least take off your sweater.

Julienne Do you think so? . . . Oh, no, see, my arms are still cold. No, no, it's the thermal vest . . .

They half turn.

Julienne Was he married to that girl?

Pierre Who?

Julienne Alex.

Pierre No.

Julienne It's funny, three of them, and none of them ever married.

9

Pierre Yes.

Julienne Especially for people of that generation. It's unusual.

Pierre I married you when I was sixty-three.

Julienne You're not a very good example. Hey, look, isn't that her over there?

Pierre puts on his glasses.

Pierre Aha!

Julienne What's she doing?

Pierre Looks like she's broken down.

They set off to meet Élisa.

4

The father's burial site.
Alex appears. He's holding the secateurs in one hand,
while in the other are three dry, chestnut-coloured thistle
stems. For a long moment, he looks at the earth. Finally,
he squats down. Pause.

Alex Listen, Dad. You don't have much choice but to
listen, what with your nostrils full of earth, no more
shouting, eh? Now it's me, shouting on my own,
shouting non-stop. When I look at myself, I feel like a
little old man. I'm shouting, snapping away like a lap-
dog, there's something pinched, here, around my mouth.
When I was twelve, you slapped me once, because I was
eating a chicken leg with one hand. No warning, you
didn't even say, 'Use two hands', you slapped me
without a word of warning. Nobody moved a muscle.
I went up to my room, sobbing like an idiot. Nathan
came up – once he'd finished eating – and said 'He's like
that because Mummy died,' my answer was: 'Fuck off,
all he has to do is die himself . . . '

Pierre has appeared. He's stopped, a few yards off,
silent.

Alex Is that you?

Pierre I'm sorry . . .

Alex You paying a visit as well?

Pierre Just doing what my old legs tell me to, you know.
They lead, I follow.

Silence.

Are those thistles for him?

Alex No.

Pierre Reminds me of your mother. She used to make wonderful bouquets out of thistles. In the summer.

Alex Yes.

Pierre I'm sorry they weren't buried next to each other.

Alex This is where he wanted to be.

Pierre I know.

Alex The most selfish idea you could imagine.

Pierre There's a lot of land, you didn't have to come this far. (*He sits down on a tree-stump.*) Can I stay or would you rather I went?

Alex No. Stay.

Pause.

Pierre How old are you now?

Alex Forty-three.

Pierre Forty-three . . . I saw you being born and now you're forty-three . . . When I was your age, everything seemed concentrated in the past, finished, gone . . . A kind of paradise consumed.

Alex Do you still feel that way?

Pierre No! . . . No, no, not any more . . .

Alex How old was I?

Pierre When I was your age? About twenty . . .

Alex You were living in New York . . .

Pierre Boston . . . Madly in love with an American woman. (*He laughs.*) . . . I had balls the size of grapefruit, they could have launched me into space!

Alex smiles.

Alex I remember the American woman.

Pierre Did you meet her?!

Alex No, but the American woman, Pierre's Yank, she was a family myth.

Pierre Is that right? It lasted six months, after six months she ran away to Florida with a toothpaste manufacturer.

Alex But you stayed on in America.

Pierre Three years . . . But without my American woman! There were others, but she was special . . .

Slight pause.

Alex How do you explain the fact my father never remarried?

Pierre He already had three children, why should he remarry?

Alex Did he have affairs?

Pierre Not to my knowledge. Possibly . . . (*Pause.*) Maybe with Madame Natti.

Alex Madame Natti? The chiropodist?

Pierre I couldn't prove it . . . Poor man, if he could hear me now!

Alex Madame Natti!

Pierre She was very nice, pretty little triangular face. Nathan suspected it as well.

Alex He did?!

Pierre I'm sure we were mistaken.

Alex Madame Natti . . .

Pierre You know, your father wasn't very . . . it wasn't one of his central preoccupations. He was your age when Lila died, I never knew him when he was young, but later on he always gave the impression of being kind of an ascetic.

Alex Apart from banging the chiropodist.

Pierre No! . . . Well, perhaps. I hope so!

Both of them contemplate the freshly covered earth in silence. Pause.

Pierre You know, at such melancholy moments – you'll think I'm ridiculous – what comes out of my mouth sometimes are lines of poetry . . . Stupid, isn't it?

Alex No . . .

Pierre Yes, it's stupid . . .

Pause.

Alex You know the hardest thing to understand? . . . I want to ask him to forgive me . . . When he was ill, I used to go and sit on his bed, I couldn't find the words, I wanted to take his hand one day, but he moved to rearrange his sheet or his blanket . . . I didn't persist . . . He said 'Going all right, is it, the criticism?' 'Yes . . .' 'Read any good books?' . . . His voice so full of bitterness! . . .

Silence.

You think I'll ever see him again? . . . You find that amusing?

Pierre No, no! It wasn't your question! . . . It wasn't your question that's making me smile . . .

Alex Then what is it?

Pierre Nothing . . . It's your way of . . . Your expression reminded me of something . . . Reminded me of certain expressions of yours when you were little . . . That's all.

Alex You mean at my age, you don't ask that kind of question any more, is that it?

Pierre No, no, that's not it at all!

Alex Yes, it is. You smiled with a slight air of commiseration, as if . . .

Pierre Absolutely not! I didn't smile with a slight air of anything . . . First of all, I didn't even smile, I . . . was 'repining' as they say in literature, I smiled through my repining . . . You're a real pain in the arse!

Alex What did I say? I didn't say a word . . .

Pierre And I say the first thing that comes into my head . . . I'm sorry.

Pause.

Alex You still haven't answered my question . . .

Pierre You really think I'm qualified to answer your question?

Alex You must have some opinion. Everyone has some opinion.

Pierre An opinion . . . yes.

Alex Well?

Pierre I think in a while this question of seeing him again will no longer arise . . . how's that for an opinion? . . .

Alex You mean when I'm dead?

Pierre Oh, no! Long before!

Alex But what I want is for you to tell me I will see him again! Shit, it's clear enough, it's simple enough, I want you to say to me: 'Yes. You will see him again.' That's what I need! It's grotesque of you not to understand that! That's what I need! It may be idiotic, I don't care what you think it is, but that's what I want to hear, I want someone to say to me: 'Yes! You are going to see him again!'

Silence.

Pierre I should point out that I understood what you were saying perfectly well . . .

Alex You know what he was always saying to me, the whole time! Aside from his insane desire to see me in the Académie Française. 'You have to settle down!' Settle down: that was his favourite expression . . . Can you imagine the kind of life that might conform to that idea?

Pierre When you see him again, you can ask him.

Alex Yes . . . (*He forces himself to smile.*) You understand, these are all things that have to be sorted out, otherwise . . .

Pierre Yes.

Alex Otherwise . . . I was never able to fight with him, he didn't listen to me . . . Not ever . . . I have no memory of his listening to me without getting impatient, without . . . calmly.

Pierre Yes . . .

Alex So if I never see him again . . . (*He breaks off, unable to go on.*)

Pierre You know, you don't have to say anything . . .

Alex I can't accept the idea, whatever you may think, not today, it just isn't possible . . .

16

Pierre Yes . . . Of course . . .

Silence.

Alex You're so bloody patient . . .

Pierre Oh, yes?

Alex Yes. You're so bloody patient.

Pierre Well, yes.

Silence.

We met Élisa down the road just now . . . Her car broke down . . . Poor thing, she was frantic. We walked back to the village, we telephoned everywhere, we couldn't find a single garage prepared to send someone out on Hallowe'en.

Alex Is she here?

Pierre Where else could she go? We brought her back, she wanted to stay sitting at the grocer's, waiting for some repair man from Gien, who'll never turn up.

Alex I haven't seen her for three years . . .

Pierre Three years . . . Long as that?

Alex Yes.

Pierre Really! . . .

Alex I wasn't expecting to see her again today . . .

Pierre Perhaps . . .

Alex No.

Pierre You don't even know what I was going to say!

Alex Yes, I do.

Pierre What was it, then?

Alex She didn't come to make me feel better, I can assure you. She didn't come for my sake . . . She came for conventional reasons. Out of respect for bourgeois tradition.

Pierre Stupid.

Alex Isn't it?

Pierre No, it's you that's stupid.

Silence.

Alex How do you manage to be so . . .

Pierre So what?

Alex So optimistic.

Pierre Optimistic . . . I'm not sure you've chosen the appropriate word.

Alex You know what I mean. Translate it for me.

Pierre You mean in life I display a certain cheerfulness . . . Yes . . . Yes . . . But when I'm dead, no one's going to come and cry on my grave because of a chicken leg.

Alex sobs.

Blackout.

5

Somewhere in the garden. Élisa, Édith and Julienne are out walking.

Julienne Who keeps it all in order? A gardener?

Édith Not any more. There used to be a gardener. Now it more or less runs itself.

Élisa I like it like this, a bit overgrown . . .

Édith Me too. After all, it's the country.

Julienne You have a big kitchen-garden, it's a shame it's not being used.

Édith It's always been used. Daddy did a lot of work on it.

Julienne It's wonderful to be able to eat your own fruit. Or vegetables. Mostly vegetables, in any event!

Édith We had strawberries. And gooseberries. But the gooseberries didn't work out very well, they were sour.

Julienne I don't like gooseberries much. Unless you put them in fruit salad, with plenty of sugar.

Édith Yes . . .

    Pause.

Julienne Honestly, you'd think it was the summer! I put a little woolly vest on this morning to be on the safe side, I had to take it off on the way back, I couldn't bear it any more.

Édith The grass is quite dry, it hasn't rained for days . . .
We can sit on the grass if you like?

Élisa Let's sit down.

Julienne Yes, let's sit down!

They sit down. Pause.

Édith Short hair suits you.

Élisa You think so?

Édith Shows off your pretty neck, it's very slender . . .

Élisa Nice of you to say so.

Julienne You used to have long hair?

Élisa Yes.

Édith She had a long plait hanging down.

Élisa When I first had it cut, I was practically bald,
I looked like Madame Vacher's son. It's better now.

Édith It's good like that.

Élisa Yes, it's good like that.

Silence.

Julienne While I think of it . . . (*She rummages in her
handbag.*) Here's the famous thermal vest, I stuffed it in
my handbag, otherwise I'd have forgotten it . . . I don't
think you've seen this, I brought you a photo of your
father taken at Saint-Jean during the wedding . . . Now
where is it? Ah, here it is! (*She hands the photo to
Édith.*) It's yours, obviously. (*Her voice full of sorrow.*)
I think it's really good.

Élisa It's beautiful . . .

Julienne Isn't it? Really 'Warm'. 'Warm', that's the word
that springs to mind.

Édith contemplates the photo.

Édith Can I keep it?

Julienne It's for you. I brought it specially.

Édith You'd think it was Nathan. The expression.

Élisa Yes, the smile . . .

Pause.

Taken during your wedding?

Julienne Yes. Taken two years ago, the date's on the back . . . I always put the date on photos, otherwise you have no idea where or when . . .

Élisa All the same, you wouldn't be likely to forget the date of your wedding!

Julienne Who knows? . . . No, of course not! But it's just one of my habits, I always put the date on documents, photos, bills, even postcards!

Élisa Do you keep them in albums?

Julienne Postcards? No!

Élisa Photos.

Julienne Oh, yes. Of course I do . . . Don't you?

Élisa No.

Julienne Don't you either, Édith?

Édith Yes, I do . . .

Julienne I have six or seven at least. Children, grand-children . . . It's my hoarding instinct, like an ant.

They smile.
Pause.

Édith Do you still see your first husband, Julienne?

Julienne My first husband's dead, poor man, he had a heart attack when he was thirty-five.

Édith I'm sorry, I had no idea.

Julienne Don't be sorry, how could you have known? After that I married a dentist, who I divorced eight years ago. We stayed on good terms, we see each other occasionally. When I married Pierre, he even sent me a congratulatory telegram.

Élisa Three husbands. If I may say so, you've done the work for all of us!

Julienne On my eighteenth birthday, a hypersensitive clairvoyant predicted I would become a nun. I was no beauty, but even so! So I launched myself, you might say, on a counter-offensive . . .

Élisa And won.

Julienne (*modestly*) Ultimately, yes.

> *Silence.*
> *Édith stares into the distance, overcome by some private suffering. Élisa and Julienne secretly watch her, not daring to say any more.*

Édith When I was little, I used to make necklaces out of daisies. Daisy-chain crowns on my head . . . In spring, the ground around here is covered in them.

Élisa Do you still see Jean?

Édith More or less . . . I'm talking about daisy-chains and you're thinking about Jean.

Élisa (*smiling*) No . . .

Édith My perennial lover . . .

> *Pause.*

22

You know what Daddy used to say: 'Your greatest success in life, the only act you can congratulate yourself on, is not to have married Jean!' . . . He used to call him Mr Tsetse Fly . . . (*She smiles.*) . . . It was so stupid! So stupid that after a while we couldn't help laughing . . . (*She can't help laughing.*) . . . 'Invite Mr Tsetse Fly, he'll put us to sleep!'

She laughs. Julienne and Élisa follow suit.

Daddy's dead, but I still have Jean. And Jean's going to London . . . I'm a dried-up old apple.

Silence.

Julienne If you're a dried-up old apple, what am I? . . .

Édith You have children, you have grandchildren, you have a husband, a family . . . You wear make-up, you get dressed up . . .

Julienne Well, nothing's stopping you wearing make-up or getting dressed up! . . .

Édith For whom?

Julienne For anyone! For everyone . . . For yourself!

Édith I'd want it to be for someone, to make myself beautiful for someone . . .

Julienne I'm sorry, Édith, but your reasoning is backwards. Wear make-up, get dressed up, and the someone will turn up within the hour! . . . (*to Élisa*) Am I talking nonsense, dear?

Élisa No . . .

Édith I spent the night with a man. One night . . . My boss, nothing could be more banal . . . One evening, I waited for him by his car, I said to him, 'I want to stay with you tonight' . . . 'All night?' he answered. I said,

'Yes' . . . (*Pause.*) I had no make-up, nothing . . . I was just as I am now . . .

Silence.

Élisa What happened?

Édith I don't know why I'm telling you this now.

Élisa Tell us anyway . . .

Édith We went to his house. He offered me a drink. He got undressed and we went to bed as if it was the most natural thing in the world . . .

Pause.

I cried . . . We spent a moment pressed against each other and then he withdrew and I retreated to the far side of the bed . . . He said, 'What's the matter?' He leant over me, he ran his hand through my hair, he touched my cheek, he said, 'Come here' . . . He lifted me up and I went back and buried myself against him . . . He said, 'What's the matter? Why are you crying? Is it my fault?' I wanted to say yes and I said no, because what his question meant was, 'Wasn't I what you wanted?' and in fact he had been, down to the least little gesture, with all his slightly weary ardour, exactly what I wanted . . .

Pause.

Élisa Did you see him again?

Édith Yes, at the office. Nothing else . . . Then he left.

Silence.

At thirty-nine . . . I was thirty-nine at the time . . . I was no lover . . . I didn't know what to do . . . This man, if he'd looked at me, perhaps I might have been able to make myself more attractive . . .

Pause.

During the burial this morning – I haven't been able to think about anything else all day – I imagined him appearing behind a tree . . . Staying slightly to one side and never taking his eyes off me . . . All women tell the same stories. There's no philosophical system behind it . . .

Élisa Are you sure? . . .

Slight pause.

Édith Why did you come?

Élisa You know why I came.

Édith No . . .

Élisa Too bad.

Édith When I saw you arriving, I thought you must be crazy . . .

Élisa Do you still think that?

Édith Yes . . .

Élisa Then why ask the question?

Édith (*to Julienne, who in spite of her embarrassment and a growing incomprehension is forcing herself to look neutral*) This woman, my dear Julienne, has driven both my brothers crazy.

Élisa Don't exaggerate.

Édith To distraction, then, if you prefer, with love! . . . Don't make that face at me, I'm not blind, you know . . .

Élisa You're wrong. I wish you were right, but you're wrong . . . (*to Julienne*) If you'll allow me to set the record straight: I simply lived with Alex and it was I who loved Nathan 'to distraction'. There . . . You must admit that's something quite different.

Julienne smiles politely.

Édith You were his mistress?

Élisa For one night . . .

Édith Does Alex know?

Élisa No. I don't think so . . . One night of love and then separation . . . (*She smiles.*) Like you and your boss . . . And you, Julienne, don't you have some night to tell us about? May I call you Julienne?

Julienne No . . . I mean, yes, obviously you can call me Julienne! . . . but I don't have a night . . . I mean, I don't have a night, er . . . of course there were nights, but I don't have that particular kind of a night . . . I'm expressing myself horribly badly all of a sudden. (*She brings a handkerchief out of her handbag, very jittery.*)

Édith We're being very rude to you.

Julienne Oh, no, not at all.

Élisa She's right, I'm sorry.

Julienne No, there's no reason to be. I'm not on the scrap-heap yet, even if I look as if I am!

Élisa That's not what I meant! Besides, that's not at all the impression you give.

Julienne I was joking. (*Slight pause.*) I'd like to make a small comment, Édith, even though my position as involuntary audience perhaps doesn't entitle me to this observation, but I find it entirely natural, entirely natural on a day like today, for you to clutch at certain memories. Clutch is an ugly word, that's not what I meant to say . . . What's the word for bumping into something . . . Bump . . . Collide?

Édith It's done me good to talk. I'm not thinking about it any more, already.

Silence.

Nathan appears, carrying a shopping-basket, from which carrots and leek stems protrude. He stops and takes a slight pause, surprised.

Nathan You came back?

Élisa My car broke down. They're going to come and fix it about six o'clock . . . You didn't see it?

Nathan I wasn't on that road, I've just come back from Dampierre. What's wrong with it?

Élisa You're asking me?!

Nathan You want me to take a look at it?

Élisa You know something about cars?

Nathan No. Nothing whatsoever.

Élisa The grocer says it's the automatic gearbox.

Nathan (*smiling*) Of course, he's an expert, Monsieur Vacher! . . . I've brought the makings of an enormous *pot-au-feu*, will you come with me, ladies?

They leave, following Nathan.

Blackout.

6

The terrace.

*Nathan appears, immediately followed by Édith,
Julienne and Élisa. He puts down the basket and empties
its contents on to the table.*

Nathan Leeks, carrots, shoulder of beef and marrow-
bones, parsley, tomatoes . . .

Édith You don't put tomatoes in a *pot-au-feu*.

Nathan We'll put them in just this once . . . gherkins,
potatoes and . . . turnips! Is that all right? I hope you're
staying for dinner?

Julienne Love to, if Pierre has no objection.

Nathan Where is he?

Julienne With your brother somewhere, I imagine. I can
start peeling the vegetables, if you like?

Nathan We can all peel them together, can't we, out
here? Make the most of the sun.

Édith I'll go and put the meat on. I'll bring some knives.
(*She leaves, taking with her the meat, the parsley and the
box of gherkins.*)

Nathan (*to Élisa*) Are you staying?

Élisa No . . .

Nathan Don't be silly, how are you planning to get
away?

Élisa I don't know. If the car really is buggered, I'll take
the train. There must be a train from Gien.

Julienne Stay, we'll take you back.

Élisa I don't think so, thanks . . .

Nathan Will you help us to peel the vegetables anyway?

Élisa (*smiling*) Yes, of course . . . You've bought enough for a regiment.

Nathan I have no sense of proportion . . . I asked the woman to give me all the necessary ingredients for a *pot-au-feu*, it was her who put the tomatoes in. You really don't put tomatoes in a *pot-au-feu*?

Élisa In principle, no.

Julienne We'll make a little salad, that'd be nice.

Nathan There we are.

Édith returns with some sheets of newspaper, some knives, a colander and two salad bowls. She puts everything on the table next to the vegetables.

Édith I'll put the water on to boil, I'll be back. (*She sets off again.*)

Élisa, Nathan and Julienne spread the paper out on the table, sit down and start peeling.

Julienne You don't have a peeler? Although it's just as quick to do it with an ordinary knife.

Nathan Want me to go and have a look?

Julienne No, no, don't bother. I'm just being fussy, I'll be perfectly fine with this.

Pierre appears, followed by Alex.

Pierre What's this? What's this?

Julienne Are you going to come and give me a hand, darling?

Pierre Is that wise?

Alex What is it?

Nathan A *pot-au-feu*.

Pierre sits at the table. Alex remains standing, motionless.

Pierre (*to Élisa*) I'm a killer at this sort of thing. I take scalps!

Alex (*to Élisa*) Has your car broken down?

Élisa Yes . . .

Alex Did you call the garage?

Élisa Yes . . . someone's coming for it about six o'clock.

Alex What's the matter with it?

Nathan Monsieur Vacher says it's the automatic gear-box!

Alex Really! . . . You have an automatic?

Élisa (*smiling*) Yes.

Alex Good . . . Practical in town, is it?

Élisa Yes . . .

Alex Practical. Good . . . (*Pause.*) Where's Édith?

Nathan In the kitchen. She's coming.

Alex Good, well . . . let's get peeling! . . . (*He sits at the table and grasps a turnip.*)

Silence. Édith arrives.

Édith Ah, you're all here!

Pierre Personally, I'm just supervising!

Édith Can you make some room for me, next to you, in the sun?

Pierre Yes, here, come!

Julienne I'm repeating what I said this morning, but, in any event, I've never seen weather like this in November!

Alex This turnip is rotten.

Julienne I must admit, these are not best quality turnips. (*to Nathan*) It's not your fault!

Nathan I can't say I feel particularly guilty.

Julienne In any case you're doing that like a real professional!

Nathan You think so?

Alex My brother's a great professional, Julienne. At everything and in every way. He's what I would call a professional personified.

Nathan This is not a compliment, you understand.

Alex Why? It is a compliment . . . (*He picks up a second turnip.*) Words are the only things which change over time . . . When I was a child, all my heroes looked like Nathan. Sinbad, D'Artagnan, my favourite Tom Sawyer, all Nathan . . . The radiant, invincible Nathan, the one exemplary being . . . Rotten as well. Completely! . . . (*He throws the turnip aside and picks up a potato.*) You know he was giving piano concerts when he was ten. In the drawing-room. The whole family used to listen religiously.

Julienne Do you still play?

Nathan I still play, but I don't give recitals any more!

Alex Ah, yes! . . . More's the pity . . . At one time, I used to play the flute . . .

Laughter.

No, no, it's true! The 'Kena' . . . A sort of hollow piece of bamboo, with holes, I bought it in the metro. It was my Cordillera period, with my llama-wool bonnet from the Andes.

Édith I don't remember hearing you play.

Alex You don't? Well, neither do I. I never managed to get a peep out of it.

Pierre And that's what you call playing the flute.

Alex Certainly. You put on a record, say the Machucambos, and you play along, in front of the mirror . . .

Nathan In a red poncho . . .

Alex Yes, and that little cagoule that suited me so well . . . Dad conducted the world's great orchestras that way.

Élisa In a poncho?

Alex No. In his pyjamas . . . Tell me, do these vegetables reduce in the stock? You've got enough here for six months!

Édith We don't have to put them all in.

Alex Are you staying to dinner? What I mean is, are you staying the night?

Pierre If it's all right with everyone, I'd just as soon leave tomorrow morning.

Édith Your room's made up, you could even stay till Monday.

Pierre No, no . . .

Julienne I didn't bring my toothbrush or my nightie.

Pierre Great!

Julienne Listen to him! . . .

Nathan You'll find everything you need here.

Julienne Thanks very much.

Élisa I need to telephone the station at Gien.

Édith It's Saturday . . . There's a train at eight.

Nathan I'll come with you.

Élisa Thank you . . .

Édith Stop! That's enough, no point in peeling the rest, otherwise I won't know what to do with it.

She gets up and starts clearing up. Élisa, Julienne and Pierre follow suit. Nathan leaves the table and moves away to light a cigarette. Only Alex stays seated.

Julienne (*to Nathan*) You know what you've forgotten? Not that it matters: an onion!

Nathan Oh, yes, sorry.

Julienne I'm teasing, but it does give it a bit of flavour!

Nathan Yes, yes.

Toing and froing. They disperse, carrying vegetables and peelings into the house. Alex and Nathan remain. Pause.

Alex . . . 'It does give it a bit of flavour!'

Édith reappears to collect the salad bowls.

Nathan Do you need me any more?

Édith No, no, there's nothing left to do . . .

She grabs the knife and the potato which Alex is still whittling away at and leaves. Nathan wanders away down the garden. Alex is alone.

Blackout.

7

The father's burial site.

Nathan is motionless, his hands in his pockets. There are thistle stalks on the ground and, not far off, the secateurs.

Silence.

Soundlessly, and as if not daring to approach, Élisa appears. There's a long pause before the dialogue.

Nathan Two weeks ago, I went into his room, he couldn't get up any more . . . He asked me to bring him the record-player and the loudspeakers, those were the expressions he used . . . I set it up beside his bed. He wanted to listen to the *Arioso* of Opus 110, Beethoven's penultimate sonata, only that passage . . . We listened in silence, he raised a finger like that, so I wouldn't speak. I was sitting on his bed. There's a fugue in the middle, then the theme starts up again . . . When the record was finished, he said to me: 'I'm convinced we're going to meet.' I asked him: 'Who?' 'Beethoven, the exemplary genius . . . A man who provides you with that kind of intuition, surely you don't think he can be dead!' Unlike Alex, I'm very happy he's buried here.

Silence.

Élisa Whose decision was it?

Nathan His. He didn't want cemeteries and funerals . . . Since he retired, he's been living here.

Élisa Even when he was ill?

Nathan Yes. He had a full-time nurse.

Pause.

Élisa And Alex?

Nathan Alex? . . .

Élisa Was he with him?

Nathan He came to see him . . . Often at the wrong time, poor sod. He'd bring him books when Dad wasn't able to read, and he moved in, at the end, when the old man couldn't recognise anybody any more . . . You've changed.

Élisa Aged.

Nathan No. Yes, perhaps.

   Silence.

Élisa Are you still at Nanterre?

Nathan No. I've been called to the bar in Paris.

Élisa Ah . . .

   Pause.

Nathan And you?

Élisa Nothing special . . .

Nathan Meaning?

Élisa Nothing. My life hasn't changed.

   Pause.

Nathan You still living at the other end of the world?

Élisa Yes.

Nathan Rue Saint-Bernard.

Élisa Yes.

Nathan Good . . .

   Élisa smiles.

It was nice what you said to me.

Élisa Thanks. Is that the word? . . .

Nathan What do you want me to say?

Élisa Nothing . . .

Nathan Your car breaking down, it's like something out of a novel.

Élisa I swear it's true.

Nathan I believe you. If you ask me, it's him, up there in heaven, who's contrived to bugger the motor around a bit.

Élisa Don't be ridiculous.

Nathan I'm not. He did it to give me pleasure . . .

Pause.

Élisa It gives you pleasure that I'm here?

Nathan What do you think? . . . Alex has forgotten the secateurs.

Silence.
Nathan picks up the secateurs and puts them in his pocket.

Why did you come?

Élisa Now?

Nathan Today.

Élisa You'd do better to ask me how I found the strength to come . . . I've never done anything so contrary to reason.

Silence.

You want me to leave you?

36

Nathan No. I don't want you to leave me . . . (*Pause.*) You're more of a forbidden fruit than ever, Élisa. But today I don't want you to leave me . . . (*Pause.*) You know what I'm thinking? Something equally contrary to reason . . . That I'd like to have you. Here. On top of his grave . . . To banish one kind of pain with another. (*She goes right up to him.*)

Élisa Let me be your pain, Nathan . . .

He kisses her passionately and starts to undress her.

Blackout.

8

The terrace.
  Alex, still at the table.
  Julienne appears, in a great rush.

Julienne Where's Élisa?

Alex She's fucking my brother.

Julienne I beg your pardon?!

Alex She's in the process of fucking my brother.

Julienne I don't understand!

Alex Yes, you do, Julienne, you understand very well.
You're not deaf, are you?

Julienne But where?!

Alex Ha! Ha! Ha! . . . What a wonderful question! Ha!
Ha! . . . Still, you're very quick on your feet!

Julienne That's not what I meant to say! . . . I meant
you're here . . . given that you're here and I've just come
out of the house . . . oh, damn it!

  She leaves, very flustered. Édith arrives.

Édith Where's Élisa?

Alex No idea.

Édith You didn't see her come out?

Alex Yes, she went that way . . .

Édith Pierre's on the phone with the garage, they can't
send anyone before Monday morning!

Alex shrugs his shoulders.

What can we do?

Alex Call someone else . . .

Édith It's the only place available. Anyway, no one does repairs on a Sunday! . . . What can we do? Shall we agree to Monday? And if we leave tomorrow evening, who are we going to leave the keys with?

Alex Do what you like, I couldn't give a flying fuck.

Édith We could leave them with Vacher, he knows where the car is. He's not closed on Monday morning, is he?

Alex I don't know. I don't give a fuck.

Édith Thanks for your help . . . (*She leaves.*)

Alex Can't she climb out of her own pile of shit?! . . . Why's she getting on our tits with her clapped-out old heap?!!

He stays seated for a moment, alone. Then gets up, turns and moves a few steps towards the woods. Pierre appears.

Pierre Where are you going?

Alex Mm?!

Pierre It's going to rain.

Alex You think so? Yes . . .

Pierre Stormy weather. That's why it's been so warm.

Alex Yes . . .

Pause.

Pierre Care for a cigarillo?

Alex You smoke cigarillos?

Pierre Once every six months . . . (*He offers the packet to Alex, who helps himself.*) Present from the concierge. Spanish cigarillos. What do you think? (*Alex coughs.*) Strong, eh?

Alex (*coughing and laughing*) It's disgusting!

Pierre Yes.

Alex It's like . . .

Pierre Cheese. *Pont-l'évêque*. Tastes like *pont-l'évêque* . . . I mean, you get used to it . . .

Alex When are you leaving?

Pierre Tomorrow morning. Is that a problem for you?

Alex No, no . . . Can you think of anything more lugubrious than the country in the autumn? . . . The silence . . . Nothing moving . . . I hate the country . . . If it was up to me, I'd sell the whole lot . . . Tomorrow.

He moves around, smoking his cigarillo. Pierre stays still.

Nathan adores the country.

Pierre You're very unfair to Nathan.

Alex In what way? Because I say he likes the country?

Pierre Among other things . . .

Alex You think that's a character flaw?

Pierre I don't, no.

Alex Nathan goes for walks, he tramps around on his own for hours . . . (*Pause.*) He meditates, among the trees.

Pierre Whereas you shout yourself hoarse in the turbulent maelstrom of life . . .

Alex smiles. Slight pause.

Everything you do badly, he does well . . . Everything you dislike makes him happy . . . To judge from what you say, he's the most respectable man on earth, and the most inhuman . . .

Alex Inhuman? No . . .

Pierre Yes. Talented, deep, uninfluenceable . . . all your rattlesnake compliments . . . no one can stand up against that, believe me.

Alex (*after a pause, as if getting his breath back*) You're on very good form, Pierrot, but you don't understand what you're talking about . . .

Pierre Nothing new about that, as you know . . . Are you cold?

Alex Freezing.

Pierre You want to go in?

Alex No.

Silence.

Three years ago, Élisa left me. At that time, everybody thought I was an idiot. A blind idiot. He undertook never to see her again. Out of friendship towards me, I imagine . . . He stood aside . . . just as he gave up music, just as he gave up his brilliance, his streak of madness, his heroism . . . I've certainly never loved anyone as much as him. If Nathan died, you can't imagine how lonely I'd be . . . as lonely as he is today, perhaps . . . But once again he says nothing. He goes shopping for dinner . . . He comes back with a ton of vegetables, and everybody sits peeling them in the sun because of him, solely because of him . . .

Édith appears. Silence.

All right?

Édith Yes . . . (*Pause.*) Who were you talking about?

Alex Nathan.

Édith What were you saying?

Alex You like the country as well, don't you?

Édith What a strange question!

Alex You don't think it's lugubrious?

Édith Today, perhaps.

Pierre With this sudden light . . .

Édith It's going to rain.

Pierre Exactly what we were saying.

Édith Be so good as not to take me for a complete fool.

Pierre What do you mean? It's true. It's exactly what we were saying.

 Pause.

Alex Have you sorted out the car business?

Pierre Yes . . . I told the man to come and fetch it on Monday. What's my wife doing?

Édith Watching TV.

Pierre What's on?

Édith I don't know. Some variety show, I don't know . . .

Pierre Good . . . I didn't even know you had a telly here, is that new?

Édith It's been here about a year . . . We had it put in for Daddy.

Pierre Oh, yes, of course . . .

 Silence.

Édith Everything's on the stove, at last. I put everything in three big pots, we'll eat the left-overs tomorrow . . . Can I have one of those little cigars?

Alex I wouldn't recommend it.

Édith Why?

Pierre Don't listen to him. (*He offers the packet to Édith*.) Here you are.

Édith Are they not good?

Alex They're out of the ordinary . . .

Édith (*smoking*) I don't mind.

They watch her smoking.

Don't look at me like that! (*She laughs.*) It looks like you've given me poison and now you're waiting for me to die!

Alex You're not far wrong . . .

Nathan appears, followed by Élisa. He's holding the secateurs and the thistle-stalks cut by Alex.
  Silence.

Nice walk?

Nathan Did you cut these?

Alex I might have left them there on purpose . . .

Nathan And the secateurs? . . . I brought everything, to be on the safe side.

Slight pause.

Alex (*to Élisa*) You were together?

Nathan Yes. Why?

Alex I'm allowed to ask a question. Why say why?

Pierre (*to Élisa*) I had the garage on the phone.

Élisa What time is it?

Pierre Calm down, just calm down! He can't come this evening. We agreed on Monday morning.

Édith Since no one will be here, I've said we'll leave the keys at the grocer's . . . Unless you can think of another solution?

Élisa I'm sorry to have been such a nuisance . . .

Pierre The only nuisance is to you! Not to mention you'll have to come back to collect it.

Élisa Yes.

Pierre Let's hope it's nothing too serious.

Élisa Yes . . .

Alex She's no longer with us . . .

Élisa What?!

Alex You're no longer with us, Élisa . . . Am I wrong?

Nathan We're all a bit distracted today. Aren't we?

Alex Absolutely!

Nathan There are times one couldn't give a damn what's happened to one's car . . .

Alex Yes, personally I couldn't give a tuppenny damn!

Nathan Well, she feels the same way.

Alex Well, great! . . . (*Pause.*) Not very nice for Pierre and Édith!

Édith (*to Élisa*) Don't listen to him.

Élisa They're speaking for me, I haven't said a word . . .

Nathan What's become of my *pot-au-feu*?

Édith It's cooking.

Nathan It's going to rain . . .

Élisa (*to Pierre*) Where's your wife?

Pierre Inside. Watching TV.

Nathan Perhaps we should join her?

Pierre Very good idea. Providing we switch the thing off . . . (*to Élisa*) Will you come with me?

Élisa goes over to Pierre who leads her away towards the house. Nathan is about to follow them when Édith intercepts him.

Édith Could you stay a minute? There's something I want to say to you . . .

Alex Am I in the way?

Édith Yes, please, I won't be long.

Alex hesitates. He takes a few steps, then turns back.

Alex (*to Édith*) By the way . . . I learned something about Dad just now, I thought it might amuse you to know about it as well . . .

Édith What?

Alex Ask him . . .

He goes up to Nathan and whispers a word in his ear. Nathan smiles.

(*to Édith*) Everyone has his secrets . . . (*He moves away.*) I'll be in my room. If anyone needs me.

Nathan (*flourishing the thistles*) What shall I do with these?

Alex Throw them away.

He disappears. Édith and Nathan are alone.

Édith Tell me.

Nathan You first . . .

Édith It's raining . . .

Nathan No . . .

Édith Yes, I felt a drop . . . Will you help me put the chairs away?

Nathan What's the matter?

Pause.

Édith You were with Élisa?

Nathan Yes.

Édith She went to find you?

Nathan Yes!

Édith Alex said to Julienne that you were fucking Élisa. I'm quoting word for word . . .

Nathan Is that what you wanted to say to me?

Édith Yes.

Nathan So?

Édith What do you mean, so?

Nathan So?

Édith So, you think that's normal?

Nathan What do you mean by normal? Is it the phrase that's disturbing you or the idea it implies?

Édith You're a monster . . .

Nathan Listen, Édith, so far today has passed off without upheavals, if I may say so . . . Will you leave those chairs alone! . . . We're civilised people, we observe the rules, everyone holds their breath, there's no tragedy . . . And why exactly? I don't know, but that's the way it is. You and I collaborate in this effort for dignity . . . We're discreet, 'elegant', we behave perfectly . . . It's not that Alex is less civilised, but his pride lives somewhere else . . . Somewhere else.

Édith Why do you defend him?

Nathan I'm not defending him . . . If he comes and tells poor Julienne that I'm fucking Élisa, that's part of his nature, but you repeating it to me, off to one side like at school, like a little girl, you being so concerned about it, today, well, that I don't understand.

    Silence.

Édith I repeated it to you so that you'd know Alex's state of mind . . . She's crazy to have come today.

Nathan No.

Édith Yes.

Nathan No, I said. You repeated it to me out of curiosity. Because you had a suspicion . . . (*He comes up to her and takes her in his arms.*) . . . Mm? . . . (*He kisses her and tenderly strokes her hair.*)

Édith Do you still love her?

Nathan That's what you wanted to say to me.

    Édith moves away. She looks around, confused. The weather's changed. Everything is grey.

Shall we go in?

Édith What were you supposed to tell me about Daddy?

Nathan (*hesitates before speaking*) You remember Madame Natti?

Édith The chiropodist?

Nathan Yes . . .

Édith What about her?

Nathan Well, it seems that Dad's chiropody sessions were perhaps . . . and this is purely supposition . . . not entirely devoted to his feet . . . You see, after all, we're not really changing the subject.

Édith Daddy . . . ?!

Nathan Daddy.

Édith With that woman . . .

Nathan She was pretty . . .

Édith She was at least thirty years younger . . .

Nathan In which case, he wasn't doing too badly . . .

Édith Did you know?

Nathan More or less.

Édith Did he tell you?

Nathan No . . . I was at his place one day, in the Rue Pierre-Demours, and Madame Natti arrived, she set up her little washbowl and laid out her scissors . . . and I left. I'd forgotten my glasses, I went back ten minutes later . . . I rang, rang again, and finally Dad arrived, slightly dishevelled, to open the door, wrapped in that yellow oilskin, you know, the yellow oilskin which hung in the front hall this last hundred years, I thought it was somewhat peculiar indoor wear . . . he gave me back my glasses through the door, without letting me back in . . .

Édith You didn't ask him anything?

48

Nathan Yes. To fetch my glasses.

Édith Why didn't you tell us?

Nathan makes an evasive gesture. Pause.

Poor man . . .

Nathan Poor man? . . . Why?

Édith Because.

They stand there a moment, both motionless.

Blackout.

Inside the house.

Armchairs, a low table. A small sideboard. Élisa, Julienne and Pierre are sitting down.

Pierre I was living in a little studio on Rue Lepic. At that time I hadn't a penny, but I did have a very rich mistress, the wife of a Dieppe lawyer who had an office in Paris. In short, the fellow travelled a lot, and one year in particular she found herself on her own over Christmas. I wasn't doing anything special, bits and pieces, and she suggested we go and spend a week in Megève. A lovers' jaunt. Why not? She says to me: 'Here's the money, you make the bookings, train tickets, hotel and so on.' I take the money and I go to a travel agent's in Rue . . . can't remember, anyway, not far from the Opéra. I book the hotel, I book the sleeper, I pay and I leave . . .

Alex appears.

Alex Keep going!

Pierre I'm telling the Paillot story, you know the one . . .

Alex Go on, go on . . .

As Pierre continues, Alex remains on his feet.

Pierre So, where was I? . . . Yes, so, I'm leaving. I walk down the street, I'm about to take a bus to the Opéra. I'm waiting, and as the bus arrives, who should I see getting off? Paillot. An old classmate I used to see from time to time, very funny, very nice – still a friend by the way – and completely broke! . . . Hello! All right? How are you? He asks me what I'm doing and I tell him I'm

off to Megève the next day. Whereupon, er . . . he wasn't
doing anything, he was a bit down, he says to me 'It's
wonderful, Megève,' and suddenly I'm saying to him:
'Well, you know . . . ' and bringing out the envelope
from the travel agent's . . . 'It's all here, everything
booked for two, travel, hotel, demi-pension, if you're
free, let's you and me bugger off tomorrow evening!'
He looks at me, he says, 'What about the girl?' 'Don't
worry, I just won't call her, out of sight, out of mind,
anyway she's starting to piss me off' And away we went!

Alex And what happened?

Pierre Well, nothing, what happened, Megève, the snow,
wonderful . . .

Alex I thought she chased after you later to get her
money back . . .

Pierre Yes, well, more or less . . . you know, she never
did get it back!

Julienne It's monstrous! Are we supposed to think that
story's funny?

Alex Why is it monstrous?

Julienne When I think of that poor woman all on her
own in Paris! (*She laughs.*)

Pierre See, you're laughing.

Julienne I shouldn't be.

Pierre Are you shocked, Élisa?

Élisa Not at all! I think it's a very funny story. And so
does Julienne, which proves it.

Julienne No, what's shocking is he never paid her back.
He could have got her a present . . . At least sent her a
bunch of flowers! A huge bunch!

Pierre I nearly sent her a postcard when we were down there, maybe I should have.

Julienne Don't make yourself out to be even more awful than you are . . . (*to Élisa*) He thinks you'll find him attractive, poor dear!

Alex Élisa's very susceptible to this sort of humour. She likes cynical and immoral men.

Pierre Steady on!

Alex Not you, poor old Pierrot, you're a choirboy. (*He moves towards the imaginary window.*) It's raining . . .

Pierre Are they still outside?

   Pause.

Julienne Strange how changeable the weather is!

Élisa Yes . . .

Alex Have you ever seen a map of the world designed by a Russian? Russia is in the centre and we're stuck up the top in a sort of deep gully . . . It's fascinating!

Pierre May we know why you're suddenly talking about this?

Alex Because I'm looking out at the country.

   Nathan arrives, drenched.

Julienne God, you're soaked!

Nathan It's nothing, nothing at all, does you good.

Pierre Where's your sister?

Nathan Gone upstairs to change.

Pierre You find us in the middle of a geography lesson!

Alex Philosophy . . .

Pierre Philosophy!

Nathan May I join in?

Alex smiles. Pause.

Nathan Well . . . all right, too bad!

Élisa You ought to change, you'll catch cold.

Nathan No, no, it'll dry . . .

Pierre I told them the Paillot story! . . .

Nathan (*to Julienne*) Hadn't you heard it?

Julienne No!

Pierre She was appalled.

Julienne Absolutely not! In any event, I don't see why I should be appalled!

Nathan It's dark . . . it's miserable here. Aren't you drinking anything? Not even a cup of tea?

Édith appears.

Édith I got changed, I was drenched . . .

Alex What about a little game to cheer us all up a bit? Mm? Monopoly, Scrabble, we have everything.

Nathan Draughts, chess . . .

Édith You're not going to play a game? No one wants to play a game!

Nathan Cluedo . . .

Alex Cluedo! Ha! Ha! The silliest bloody game in the world! . . . What made you think of that?!

Nathan I'm afraid Julienne might not know the rules.

Alex Of course she does, Colonel Mustard . . .

Nathan Professor Plum . . .

Julienne Mrs Peacock . . .

Alex There you are!

Pierre You know this game?

Julienne Of course I do. What do you take me for, an idiot, you forget I have two grandchildren.

Nathan And you play Cluedo with them?

Julienne Cluedo, snakes and ladders, snap . . .

Édith How old are they?

Julienne Three and seven. Of course, I only play with the older one. The little one's only just started to talk. He says, 'Daddy', he says . . . Not that it means much, because children are more . . . I mean, at the end of the day, children who are late starters are often the most talkative!

Alex Then you must have started pretty late, did you?

Élisa Alex!

Alex What?! . . . What is it, Élisa?

Élisa Nothing . . .

Alex Yes! You said 'Alex!' What is it?

Silence.

Élisa Calm down . . .

Alex I'm quite calm. Do I seem agitated?

Édith Right, that's enough now . . .

Alex What do you mean, 'That's enough!'? What's going on? You're really pissing me off!

Nathan You must be a late starter as well . . . Although in your case the evidence isn't very conclusive.

Alex In any event! . . . Oh, Julienne, you absolutely have to explain to me the meaning of that phrase! You use it so often, you've infected me with it what's more, but I still can't grasp the, what should I call it, its 'etymology' . . .

Pierre That's a shaming admission for a literary critic.

Alex That's why I absolutely have to find out about it!

Élisa Stop it, Alex . . .

Alex You want me to stop it?

Élisa Yes.

Alex Then I'll stop it.

Pause.

Édith Go and make us a coffee, since you're so good at it.

Nathan No, herbal tea!

Alex Herbal tea? Drop of herbal tea, Julienne? I was joking. I was joking! A drop of herbal tea for everyone?

Édith Go away!

Alex I'm going. (*He leaves.*) I'm going.

Silence.

Nathan He was joking, Julienne . . . You mustn't take him seriously.

Julienne It's nice of you, but I don't think your brother likes me at all.

All He does!

Julienne (*on the brink of tears*) No, no, but it doesn't matter, it doesn't matter at all . . .

Édith Julienne, he's not his normal self today . . .

Julienne I know, I know that! Naturally, you're all very upset today, and I'm just stuck here like a . . . (*She's crying.*) Pierre insisted I came, but I'm like a stranger, I'm not really part of this family . . .

Élisa If there's someone here who's not part of this family, it's me, Julienne. Not you. You're their aunt, of course you're part of the family . . .

Julienne (*in tears*) He said things to me just now . . . As if I was some brute beast . . .

Nathan What did he say to you?

Julienne Nothing . . . He was making fun of me, that's all . . . Don't tell him, Édith, I beg of you!

Édith I'll go and look for him.

She leaves.

Julienne No! Why's she going to look for him? Leave him in peace, poor man . . .

Pierre What a day, my dears!

Julienne I'm so sorry . . . I'm so sorry, I'm ridiculous . . .

Nathan You have no reason to be sorry.

Julienne You're doing everything you can to . . . And I just start crying! . . . Like an idiot . . . (*She sobs.*) That's all I can find to do!

Édith comes back, followed by Alex. Alex stops in front of Julienne, not saying anything.

(*to Alex*) It's not your fault . . . It's all over. I'm sorry, everybody.

Alex takes hold of Julienne's arm and raises her up. When she's on her feet, he takes her in his arms, embraces her and holds her for a time, pressed against him.

When he lets her go, Julienne's face is streaked with tears.

Pause.

Pierre (*to Alex*) You wouldn't have something to drink a bit stronger than herbal tea?

Alex Yes . . . Of course! . . .

Élisa Can I come with you?

Alex Nowhere to go, it's all here.

Assisted by Nathan, he opens the door of the sideboard and brings out some bottles which he puts on the low table.

Nathan You're spoilt for choice, my friends . . . I particularly recommend the green bottle. Distilled from Hungarian artichokes . . .

Pierre It's a liqueur!

Nathan It's whatever you want it to be. You can take it with water, or ice, you can poison your wife with it!

Pierre No, we'll let her live!

Nathan Taste it, you'll see.

Pierre Is it disgusting?

Nathan A client brought it back for me. It's been there fifteen years.

Pierre Go on, give me a whisky!

Nathan Julienne?

Julienne A drop of port . . .

Alex pours it for her.

Thanks. When. You're very kind.

Nathan Élisa?

Élisa Give me a taste of the Hungarian stuff.

Pierre Ah, I was sure of it! I was sure someone would taste it and I was sure it was going to be you!

Élisa Why, do I look like someone who drinks artichoke liqueur?

Pierre You look like a pioneer! Especially your eyes . . . You have adventurous pupils!

Édith What are you talking about!

Pierre No. It's true. You like taking risks. You don't like anyone dictating the way you behave. Am I wrong?

Élisa (*smiling*) In fact, I don't have the feeling I'm taking much of a risk!

Nathan (*handing her the glass*) Don't speak too soon . . .

Élisa (*raising her glass*) We shall see what we shall see . . .

Édith What about me, you're not offering me a drink?

Alex What would you like?

Édith White port. (*to Pierre*) You're drinking it like that? Wouldn't you like some ice?

Pierre No, no, don't worry. This is perfect.

Alex and Nathan serve themselves. Élisa tastes the artichoke liqueur.

Nathan Well?

Élisa . . . It's sweet, full of nostalgia and red pepper . . .

She empties the glass.

Nathan Another?

Élisa Yes . . . You only just covered the bottom of the glass.

He pours some more for her. Élisa smiles at Pierre.
Pause.
Sound of the rain falling.

Pierre
'O pallid seasons, queens who rule our clime,
Nothing is sweeter to a death-filled mind,
Long in the grip of frosts, but than to find
Your pale gloom stretching infinite through time,
– Unless it be, one moonless night, we twain,
To reach some unsafe bed and numb our pain.'

Nathan Who's that by?

Pierre It's called 'Mists and Rains' . . . Guess.

Édith It's by you.

Pierre 'O ends of autumn, winters, mud-stained springs,
Comatose seasons! . . . ' I'm very honoured, my dear, but
it's by Monsieur Charles Baudelaire.

Nathan Tell me, Julienne, does he often bestow these
little poems on you of an evening?

Julienne Sometimes. It happens. Except it's usually in the
mornings!

Pierre In the morning, Victor Hugo! In the evening,
Baudelaire or Apollinaire . . . You're going to miss your
train, Élisa.

Nathan There's plenty of time, the train is at eight.

Alex *(to Élisa)* Why are you going back?

Élisa Because I don't want to spend the night here . . .

Alex Why?

Élisa Because . . .

Alex Because what?

Élisa Because I have to get back . . .

Alex Is someone waiting for you?

Élisa No . . .

Alex Well, then.

Slight pause.

Élisa (*smiling*) If I overdo it with the artichoke liqueur, I'll end up staying!

Alex Do you want to stay?

Élisa Listen, Alex, I've decided to leave, I'm taking the eight o'clock train and that's it!

Alex But I don't understand why you want to leave . . . Is it because of me?

Élisa No . . .

Alex (*to Pierre*) You could take her back tomorrow morning?

Pierre Of course!

Alex You can go back with them tomorrow morning, what's the problem?

Élisa I don't understand why you're insisting . . .

Alex Suppose I ask you to stay?

Élisa Why?

Alex You need a reason?

Édith For God's sake, let her do what she wants! Why flog it to death?

Élisa Thank you, Édith . . .

Alex I'm the one you should be thanking. Get that straight.

Pierre Why don't you let the girl make up her own mind? (*to Élisa*) Make your decision at the last minute, like a sensible person!

Élisa I second the motion . . .

Pierre You're very quiet, Nathan!

Nathan The discussion is closed, isn't it?

Pierre I didn't know your father was a writer. I'm completely changing the subject, but I never knew Simon wrote. It was a revelation to me this morning, when you read that piece . . .

Nathan He wrote when he was young . . . I don't think he persevered with it.

Pierre If ever there was a man . . .

Nathan You couldn't imagine being a writer . . .

Pierre Yes! It's almost a contradiction in terms . . . A mind as fundamentally abstract as his, inclined towards mathematics and music, it's impossible to imagine him giving himself over to literature!

Alex I fail to see the contradiction.

Pierre It's in the act itself . . . The physical commitment, the emotional commitment . . . Anyway, I know what I mean! (*He leans over and pours some whisky into his glass.*) Oh, old age! We say such stupid things when we're old!

Julienne You don't think we ought to take a glance at the *pot-au-feu*, do you, Édith?

Édith Everything's fine. I checked it on the way back in.

Pierre (*to Alex*) That's why he was in such despair about you not becoming a writer . . .

Alex Well now, see, this was the conclusion I was waiting for as soon as you started and all the time I was hoping it wouldn't arrive.

Pierre Wrong again!

Alex Yes, wrong again.

Pierre I'm sorry! None of this matters at all. It's the monsoon out there.

Alex I have nothing to say. I never have had anything to say. How can you be a writer when, strictly speaking, you have nothing to say?

Pierre I don't believe you have nothing to say . . .

Alex Oh, you don't? . . . You think I do have something to say? What? Tell me, what, we'll save a lot of time.

Pierre You know what, old chap, I'm tired. I don't have the strength to bugger about.

Alex You tell me I have something to say. I'm asking you what? If you know better than I do?

Édith If you have nothing to say, why don't you shut up! I can't see why you're being such a pain in the arse!

Alex Pow! . . . Such language from sweet little Édith, I didn't know you could be like that . . .

Édith Well, now you know.

Alex Yes, now I know . . . Have you made a decision, Élisa? It's no use looking at Nathan. I'm sure he wants you to stay . . .

Édith If she's staying, we'll have to light the stove in the downstairs bedroom, it's running with damp.

Nathan No point. Honestly.

Pause.

If Élisa stays, she won't be using that bedroom.

Édith Then which one will she use?

Nathan Mine.

Édith And which one will you use?

Nathan Mine as well, what do you expect? To put it another way, we'll spend the night together . . . If Élisa stays!

Silence.

Édith I think I must be dreaming . . . (*to Élisa*) What are you going to do?! Say something!

Silence.

Well, say something! Everyone making decisions for you and you're stuck there like a slab of marble! Speak!

Nathan I can't see why you're getting in this state . . .

Édith I don't understand any of this! I feel like I'm living in a lunatic asylum! . . . On the day of Daddy's burial!

She's crying.

Nathan Exactly.

Édith What do you mean, exactly?

Nathan On the day of Daddy's burial . . .

Édith You're obliged to sleep with this whore?! . . . Can't you say something, Élisa? I'm begging you, say something! . . . Daddy . . . Daddy, come back! . . . I want to die . . .

Julienne (*taking her in her arms*) Calm down, Édith, calm down . . .

Élisa Alex, drive me to the station, please.

Alex You're wrong . . .

Élisa Please . . .

Nathan I'll drive you.

Élisa Let's go . . . (*She gets up.*)

Alex Wait! (*Silence.*) One minute? I have something to say. Just one word . . . Well, perhaps a little more than one word . . . (*Pause.*) On this day of mourning . . . there was something missing . . . some event, some speech . . . In this room, there was someone I believed to be gone for good . . . who has just proved the opposite . . . That's all. (*to Élisa*) Now you can do what you like.

Élisa Are you sure that's all?

Alex She's crying . . . You're leaving . . . (*He turns to Nathan and stares at him.*) I on the other hand have an immense feeling of gratitude . . . That really is all. (*to Pierre*) Any chance of a cigar?

Pierre offers him the packet. Alex helps himself.

Édith Me too, please . . .

Alex See, there's something about these cigars . . .

He lights Édith's cigar and hands the packet back to Pierre. Pause.

Nathan (*to Élisa*) I'm still at your disposal . . .

Élisa We'll go. (*She moves towards Pierre, extending her hand.*) Goodbye . . .

Pierre Take an umbrella!

Élisa Yes . . . Goodbye, Julienne . . .

Julienne Goodbye, Élisa . . .

Élisa Did I have a coat?

Édith It's hanging in the hall cupboard . . .

Élisa leans forward, furtively kisses Édith and turns to leave.

Alex What about me, you're not going to say goodbye to me?

Élisa Goodbye . . .

Édith catches hold of Élisa's arm.

Édith Don't go . . .

Slight pause.

Alex Are we hoping to achieve a peak of ridiculousness? (*to Élisa*) Two false exits in one day, that's going it a bit, isn't it?

Édith Don't go, for pity's sake . . . I haven't the strength to speak . . .

Élisa Twice is a lot, Édith, he's right . . .

Pierre You haven't left the room yet . . .

Alex You sticking your oar in as well!

Pierre I'm not interfering. I'm making a comment . . .

Élisa (*to Alex*) Help me . . .

Alex That's what I've been doing . . . I've been watching you, you know, since this morning. I know everything about you, your gestures, your face, the way you move, the way you speak . . . I know exactly how you'll leave the room, how you'll close the door and pull on your coat . . . You won't say anything in the car, you'll light a cigarette . . . you'll pretend to be sad . . . And I don't care, I couldn't care less . . . I was expecting to be distraught, if I'd seen you again under any other circumstances, I would certainly have run after my illusions . . . Go on, bugger off!

Élisa recoils, she moves past Nathan and leaves. Nathan's getting ready to follow her, then he stops and turns back towards Alex. He's searching for what he wants to say . . . Finally, with a gesture of impotence, he smiles.

Nathan You've aged a lot today . . . You'd better watch yourself!

Alex smiles. Nathan leaves.
Silence.
Alex takes a few steps and sits down in Élisa's seat.

Alex No word from the philosopher?

Pierre Am I the philosopher?

Alex Pierrot the philosopher . . . (*to Édith*) Stop crying. Blow your nose, it's all over.

Édith I've ruined everything . . .

Alex You haven't . . .

Édith Yes, I have . . .

Alex You haven't!

Silence.

All right, Julienne?

Julienne Yes, yes . . .

Alex Families, not much fun, eh?

Julienne Listen, Alex, please, stop talking to me as if I was mentally defective . . .

Alex Well, all right!

Julienne It's extremely unpleasant, I assure you.

Alex You think they were right to leave?

Julienne What a question!

Alex There's no catch in it. I'd just be curious to hear your opinion.

Julienne I don't know, what is it you're expecting me to say?

Alex The Peugeot's at the end of the drive, they'll be soaked . . . Élisa'll be furious, her hair goes all frizzy when it rains . . . (*Pause.*) I feel good . . . I feel absolutely empty and good.

Silence.

Pierre Empty . . . Yes.

Alex Where did you two meet?

Pierre Oh, dear, oh, dear . . . Where was it?

Julienne sighs.

Through the personal columns.

Julienne Over my dead body . . .

Pierre Underneath the arcades in the Palais-Royal . . .

Julienne At a mutual friend's, boring as that.

Alex Was it love at first sight? . . .

Pierre For her, yes.

Julienne You know, you're really tiring.

Pause.

Pierre She was wearing a tam-o'shanter . . .

Julienne A tam-o'shanter!

Pierre What d'you call it? A cloak?

Julienne A cloak! A tam-o'shanter's a hat, you buffoon.

Pierre All right, then, a cloak, and we were in fact walking underneath the arcades in the Palais-Royal, without my being able to take her arm for a single second, given the shape of the garment! . . .

Julienne You could easily have taken my arm, all I needed was to bring it out.

Pierre Ah, but you didn't . . .

  Silence.

Alex Go on . . . I love these stories.

Pierre The memory's little delicacies . . .

Alex More . . . indulge me.

Julienne Little delicacies! . . . When he's on form, I say when he's on form, what I mean is when there's a big enough audience and they're paying attention, obviously, he's capable of making up the most terrible stories about us. I've heard him tell stories, not only with no beginning or end, but stories which, on top of everything else, finally make us look ridiculous.

Pierre You know what she does when that happens? She says, 'No! What are you talking about?' What's it look like?

Julienne Absolutely not. I never say anything.

Pierre You make a face . . . which is worse.

Julienne Not at all.

  Silence.

Alex More . . .

Pierre More?

Alex More . . .

Pierre Not a big enough audience, you know . . . (*He smiles.*) Shortage of spectators! (*to Édith, who has got up*) Where are you going?

Édith To the kitchen. (*She leaves.*)

Pierre (*to Julienne*) Perhaps you should go and help her . . . Don't leave her on her own . . .

Julienne gets up.

Julienne Is your brother coming back? . . . What are we going to do with that great big *pot-au-feu* if there's only four of us?

Pierre We'll give it to the cats.

Julienne (*to Alex*) You have a cat?!

Pierre There must be stray cats, wandering about . . .

Julienne leaves.

She can't bear the idea of waste. She's not particularly domestic, but the idea of waste, she's just like that . . . Are you in a dream?

Alex Am I in a dream? . . .

Flowing water is heard and a regular clattering sound. Alex is stretched out in the armchair, his eyes half closed.

Pierre What's making that noise?

Alex The gutter.

Pierre Ah . . .

Alex I tied it up with rags, practically killed myself. Didn't you see it?

Pierre Yes, yes, I saw it.

Silence.

Is your sister still seeing the . . . I can't remember his name, the wine merchant?

Alex Jean Santini. Yes.

Pierre Is he Corsican?

Alex Italian . . . By origin.

Pierre I had an accountant called Santini. He was Corsican.

Alex Oh, yes . . .

Pierre Extremely Corsican . . . You're sure this fellow isn't Corsican?

Alex Positive.

Pierre So, it's still going on . . . I didn't dare ask her today, it seemed a bit . . . I must say, your gutter's in a really bad way!

Alex I like it . . . I like the sound . . .

Pierre Yes . . . Well . . .

Silence.

Oh, it's so wonderful, being old . . . Sod it!

Silence.
Julienne returns.

Julienne (*to Pierre, under her breath*) She's crying . . .

Pierre (*after a pause*) Édith!

Alex Leave her alone . . . There's nothing you can do . . .

Julienne She wants to be alone . . . We have to leave her alone . . . Are there no other lights in here? Why don't you switch on this lamp? Is it working?

Alex Try it . . .

Julienne switches on the lamp.

Julienne That's better, isn't it?

Pierre Sit down.

Julienne I'm going to take the glasses out.

Pierre We'll do it later.

Julienne All right.

Pierre You have to keep moving, don't you?

Julienne No, no, I'm sitting down.

Pause.

What's that drumming sound?

Pierre The gutter.

Julienne The gutter's making that noise?

Pierre Yes.

Pause.

Julienne I picked up this shawl in the front hall, I can't say it goes very well . . . Don't you think it's cold? And I checked, the radiators are on.

Pierre It's the damp.

Julienne Definitely. The walls are damp.

Édith arrives, very distressed.

Édith There's someone at the door . . . Someone's trying to get in! Can you hear?!

Slight pause. Nathan and Élisa come into the room.

Nathan It's us . . . (*Pause. To Élisa*) Come on.

He takes her by the arm. They both approach.

We saw a shadow flitting past in the corridor. Was that you?

Édith I heard the lock . . . I thought someone was forcing the door . . .

Nathan It wasn't locked, we just opened it.

Édith I heard a noise.

Slight pause.

Pierre You came back . . . or you never left?

Nathan We left . . . and we came back. (*to Élisa*) Sit down.

Élisa sits down nervously.
Silence.

Julienne She's frozen stiff, poor little thing! (*She gets up and hands Élisa the shawl.*) Here, wrap yourself up in this . . . I'm sorry, Édith, I found it in the front hall, I imagine it must be yours.

Édith (*to Élisa*) Are you cold? Do you need a sweater? I've plenty of things upstairs.

Élisa No, no, not at all. Thanks. This'll do fine.

She puts the shawl around her shoulders and smiles at Édith. Édith smiles back.

It smells good when you come back . . .

Édith Does it?

Élisa Oh, yes. Very good.

Pause.
Élisa looks at Alex.

Two false exits.

Alex In one day . . . Why not?

Silence.

Pierre So you really did leave and come back? (*to Julienne*) What? I'm not asking a question! . . . My wife's very disapproving, but I'm not asking any questions!

Nathan We left this house . . . Yes . . . Édith? . . . Come closer . . . What are you doing over there? . . . We walked across the garden in the rain . . . We got in the car . . . I switched on the engine . . . I turned on the windscreen-wipers . . . and the lights . . . Élisa said nothing . . . She didn't light a cigarette, she didn't even pretend to be sad . . . We stayed where we were for perhaps a minute? . . . During the minute, something strange and sudden occurred . . . Gien Station, which we imagine to be in Gien, was there, at the end of the drive . . . the clock on the facade showed seven o'clock, we had an hour to kill . . .

Pause.
He paces up and down, Crosses to the window . . .
Then he turns back.

There were all kinds of people on the forecourt, shadows with luggage, silhouettes of drivers, taxis, hotel lights, sounds of streetcars braking in puddles . . . I said to Élisa, 'Let's go to a café . . . ' I don't remember what we ordered . . . I told her something I'd remembered from this very station about thirty years ago, and she said to me, 'I loathe stations' . . . We agreed this sensation of not being anywhere had to with evening and the provinces . . . And while we were talking, the hands on the clock turned and the hour trickled away . . . We crossed the road, we rushed to the booking-office to buy the ticket . . . then the platform, the whistle, the first carriage where she got on . . . There was the slamming of doors, that grinding of iron and the train

73

was gone . . . I watched it disappear into the countryside, and she, from her window, watched the countryside melt away . . . And the station disappeared as well . . . I switched off the engine, turned out the lights and we set off back the way we came, running as fast as we could . . .

Silence.

Alex (*to Pierre*) Now do you know why I never became a writer? . . . Precisely because of this . . . This sort of thing . . . When I get to this point, the page has always stayed blank . . . (*to Élisa*) You left . . . We stayed here, all four of us, sitting here, within these four walls, me here, in this same spot, I didn't move . . . And then, another strange thing happened, very strange . . . I was sitting in the Peugeot, in the back, you were in front, Nathan was driving, he'd turned on the windscreen-wipers double-speed, I remember this particularly, the rubber's perished, they make a scraping noise . . . we went through Dampierre and you put on a cassette . . . you put on a cassette and it was a Schubert quintet . . . You turned round and asked me if it was too loud and I said, 'No, no, no, no . . . don't change anything, whatever you do, don't change a thing.' You didn't change anything and I tipped back my head and watched the trees, the flowing lights, the drops of water bursting against the windows, Nathan's expression in the rear-view mirror, Nathan's contented expression, and the night . . . The fog and the night . . . And I was, how can I put it, emptied, weightless in the back seat, trusting, protected, a sense of indescribable well-being . . .

Pause.

. . . That's exactly what writing is, going somewhere you're not going . . . And already there, no matter what you do, already there on the blank page, is the return,

74

the end of the adventure . . . When I was twenty, I used to imagine my complete works, seven volumes on India paper, a world of giants, tempestuous, borne aloft by the swell, a prey to God knows what kind of frenzy . . . Tumultuous beings, beings capable of ingesting the world, all-inclusive, full of genius and strength and exhaustion . . . That's how coruscating I was when I was twenty . . . And instead of all that, came the everyday fixtures and fittings, the small wound at the centre of the world, the interminable flow of desires and journeys and useless gestures . . . The labyrinth of useless pathways . . . Not to mention sensitivity . . . paralysing sensitivity . . . (*Pause.*) And the superlative *pot-au-feu* which Édith has prepared for us and which I intend to sprinkle with every living spice in the kitchen!

Édith Just try it!

Alex You'll see!

Silence.

Édith I telephoned Jean just now. He's on his way.

Alex Mr Tsetse Fly is coming to dinner?

Édith Mr Tsetse Fly is coming to spend the night . . . He won't get here till midnight.

Pierre 'One moonless night, we twain . . . '

Julienne Stop it, Pierre. Shut up, just this once.

Pause.

Alex Let's go and eat!

Élisa Already?

Alex You mean at last!

Blackout.